90-DAY PERSONAL GROWTH JOURNAL

CELEBRATE YOUR
GROWTH WITH EVERY
MOMENT YOU TAKE A
STEP, NO MATTER HOW
SMALL.
-S. KANANI HAIOLA

Napualii Publishing LLC.
PO Box 4856
Kaneohe, HI 96744
http://www.napualii.com

Ordering Information

Quantity sales. Special discounts are available for quantity purchases by
corporations, associations, educational institutions, and others. For details,
contact the "Bulk Sales Department" at the Napuali'i Publishing address above.

ISBN: 978-0-9965390-4-3

Your First Seven Days

Whether you have been involved with the personal development industry or you are brand new to this, the first concept to realize is that your first seven days sets you up to accomplish your first month and then 90 days. I do not recommend that you start using this journal right away unless you already have a time that you know works for you to write in a journal. I recommend that you take the first seven days to evaluate your schedule and when you already find yourself studying and self-reflecting. Some days will be different than others. By reflecting on your schedule, it is easier to fit in a new habit with something similar you are doing and the time you are doing it in.

If you have your schedule laid out, skip ahead. If you don't, I highly recommend going through the evaluation pages that follow. Fill in the evaluation pages based on your current planner or calendar for the next week and evaluate what actually happened.

Start Date: _____

Evaluate the following for a week to find your natural rhythm. If you don't find consistent enough answers to help in your evaluation and planning, use the back of this page or add a separate blank paper to continue evaluation for an additional week.

Date:							
How did you feel waking up? (Scale 1-10)							
What time(s) in the morning and for how long did you do personal study, development, and personal writing?							
What time(s) in the evening and for how long did you do personal study, development, and personal writing?							
How do you feel before sleeping? (Scale 1-10)							
At about what time in the day did you feel complete with steps toward goals accomplished? (Put the time or n/a)							
Did the day matter? (Y/N)							

Reflections and Thoughts:

_____

_____

_____

_____

_____

_____

_____

_____

_____

_____

_____

_____

_____

_____

_____

What are your strengths from your schedule?

_____

_____

_____

_____

_____

What are your weaknesses?

_____

_____

_____

_____

_____

List a few topics you can start your personal growth journey with based on what you reflected on.

__Example: self-management, balance in scheduling__

What do you hope to gain by starting this personal growth journal?

How to use journal

Date/Time and Location: Evaluating how you keep to your same schedule and where you are that works best for keeping a journal helps in future journal entries.

Topic of Study: Focus your study on a topic, concept, or principle. It can be based on character development or areas of your well-being from health to career. Number your journal pages only the way you want and record that page number and topic on the topic index page. This makes it easier to track and for future referencing and review.

Resources/References: Name the book, page numbers, audio, video, definitions, and any other resources used to study.

Pictures/Diagrams/Notes: Some people prefer to take notes while studying. Others prefer drawing out what and how they see things. Draw something to catch your attention to the topic.

Key Thoughts/Learning: Summarize the key points and what stood out to you. Some may be new and others may be a review.

Rate yourself: The end of the day does not have to fall in line with the normal morning and night. It can be whatever time is set by you to write daily. The next day is the next writing period on the following day. At the end of your day and after you have studied, rate yourself to find improvement. This is done through rating yourself on a scale and answering the questions on applying the thoughts for the day and the small step achieved towards the application process.

Tips in developing yourself

*Developing yourself takes time so don't expect to accomplish each thought to be applied in one day. Just consider and be happy with the smallest step, even if it's a thought or a potential small hop.

*Keep doing what you have already accomplished, yet add on step by step. If you improved on smiling more, then keep smiling while applying your next development goal.

*The idea of personal growth is to add on to your growth and develop to be more full and complete. If you can't add on the next topic to what you have already accomplished, continue with the previous thought and find a way to bridge the leap into a smaller step toward adding the next.

*You may decide to take one concept or topic to master for an entire week or just one day, depending on how much you feel you need to improve and the small steps accomplished.

*Be honest and have integrity with yourself.

*If you know you work best with a partner and companion, consider who you are open with and talk to the most. Request that person to be there for you to share your development with them.

*Celebrate in some way each day and be grateful for each step that was accomplished!

"Develop yourself in all areas of well-being everyday so you can shine like the individual gem that you are."

-S. Kanani Haiola

Topic Index

Record and search the topics you develop in.

Topic	Page (s)

Topic	Page (s)

Topic	Page (s)

Topic	Page (s)

Page _____

Date/Time: _____

Location: _____

Topic of Study: _____

Resources/References: _____
_____
_____
_____
_____

Pictures/Diagrams/Notes:

Key Thoughts/Learning:

_____
_____
_____
_____

Key Thoughts/Learning (cont.):

_____
_____
_____
_____
_____
_____
_____
_____
_____

On a scale of 1-10 (10 being the best), how well are you applying the topic of study already? _____

How can I apply these thoughts and concepts today and consistently in the future?

_____
_____
_____
_____

End-of-Day Evaluation:

Rate yourself on how much you improved? _____

Small step achieved today: _____
_____
_____
_____
_____

Did today matter? _____

I am grateful for _____

Page _____

Date/Time: _____

Location: _____

Topic of Study: _____

Resources/References: _____
_____
_____
_____
_____

Pictures/Diagrams/Notes:

Key Thoughts/Learning:

_____
_____
_____
_____

Key Thoughts/Learning (cont.):

_____
_____
_____
_____
_____
_____
_____
_____

On a scale of 1-10 (10 being the best), how well are you applying the topic of study already? _____

How can I apply these thoughts and concepts today and consistently in the future?

_____
_____
_____
_____

End-of-Day Evaluation:

Rate yourself on how much you improved? _____

Small step achieved today: _____

_____
_____
_____
_____

Did today matter? _____

I am grateful for _____

Page _____

Date/Time: _____

Location: _____

Topic of Study: _____

Resources/References: _____
_____
_____
_____
_____

Pictures/Diagrams/Notes:

Key Thoughts/Learning:

_____
_____
_____
_____

Key Thoughts/Learning (cont.):

_____

_____

_____

_____

_____

_____

_____

_____

_____

On a scale of 1-10 (10 being the best), how well are you applying the topic of study already? _____

How can I apply these thoughts and concepts today and consistently in the future?

_____

_____

_____

_____

End-of-Day Evaluation:

Rate yourself on how much you improved? _____

Small step achieved today: _____

_____

_____

_____

_____

Did today matter? _____

I am grateful for _____

Page _____

Date/Time: _____

Location: _____

Topic of Study: _____

Resources/References: _____
_____
_____
_____
_____

Pictures/Diagrams/Notes:

Key Thoughts/Learning:

_____
_____
_____
_____

Key Thoughts/Learning (cont.):

_____
_____
_____
_____
_____
_____
_____
_____
_____

On a scale of 1-10 (10 being the best), how well are you applying the topic of study already? _____

How can I apply these thoughts and concepts today and consistently in the future?

_____
_____
_____
_____

End-of-Day Evaluation:

Rate yourself on how much you improved? _____

Small step achieved today: _____

_____
_____
_____
_____

Did today matter? _____

I am grateful for _____

Page _____

Date/Time: _____

Location: _____

Topic of Study: _____

Resources/References: _____
_____
_____
_____
_____

Pictures/Diagrams/Notes:

Key Thoughts/Learning:

_____
_____
_____
_____

Key Thoughts/Learning (cont.):

_____
_____
_____
_____
_____
_____
_____
_____
_____

On a scale of 1-10 (10 being the best), how well are you applying the topic of study already? _____

How can I apply these thoughts and concepts today and consistently in the future?

_____
_____
_____
_____

End-of-Day Evaluation:

Rate yourself on how much you improved? _____

Small step achieved today: _____

_____
_____
_____
_____

Did today matter? _____

I am grateful for _____

Page _____

Date/Time: _____

Location: _____

Topic of Study: _____

Resources/References: _____
_____
_____
_____
_____

Pictures/Diagrams/Notes:

Key Thoughts/Learning:

_____
_____
_____
_____

Key Thoughts/Learning (cont.):

_____
_____
_____
_____
_____
_____
_____
_____
_____

On a scale of 1-10 (10 being the best), how well are you applying the topic of study already? _____

How can I apply these thoughts and concepts today and consistently in the future?

_____
_____
_____
_____

End-of-Day Evaluation:

Rate yourself on how much you improved? _____

Small step achieved today: _____

_____
_____
_____
_____

Did today matter? _____

I am grateful for _____

Page _____

Date/Time: _____

Location: _____

Topic of Study: _____

Resources/References: _____
_____
_____
_____
_____

Pictures/Diagrams/Notes:

Key Thoughts/Learning:

_____
_____
_____
_____

Key Thoughts/Learning (cont.):

_____
_____
_____
_____
_____
_____
_____
_____
_____

On a scale of 1-10 (10 being the best), how well are you applying the topic of study already? _____

How can I apply these thoughts and concepts today and consistently in the future?

_____
_____
_____
_____

End-of-Day Evaluation:

Rate yourself on how much you improved? _____

Small step achieved today: _____

_____
_____
_____
_____

Did today matter? _____

I am grateful for _____

Congratulations
on your first week of
developing yourself!

**Go back through your first week and reflect on times and locations that has been working for you. Make sure you keep those as consistent as possible for the rest of your journey.

KEEP GOING!

Page _____

Date/Time: _____

Location: _____

Topic of Study: _____

Resources/References: _____
_____
_____
_____
_____

Pictures/Diagrams/Notes:

Key Thoughts/Learning:

_____
_____
_____
_____

Key Thoughts/Learning (cont.):

_____
_____
_____
_____
_____
_____
_____
_____

On a scale of 1-10 (10 being the best), how well are you applying the topic of study already? _____

How can I apply these thoughts and concepts today and consistently in the future?

_____
_____
_____
_____

End-of-Day Evaluation:

Rate yourself on how much you improved? _____

Small step achieved today: _____

_____
_____
_____
_____

Did today matter? _____

I am grateful for _____

Page _____

Date/Time: _____

Location: _____

Topic of Study: _____

Resources/References: _____
_____
_____
_____
_____

Pictures/Diagrams/Notes:

Key Thoughts/Learning:

_____
_____
_____
_____

Key Thoughts/Learning (cont.):

_____
_____
_____
_____
_____
_____
_____
_____
_____

On a scale of 1-10 (10 being the best), how well are you applying the topic of study already? _____

How can I apply these thoughts and concepts today and consistently in the future?

_____
_____
_____
_____

End-of-Day Evaluation:

Rate yourself on how much you improved? _____

Small step achieved today: _____

_____
_____
_____
_____

Did today matter? _____

I am grateful for _____

Page _____

Date/Time: _____

Location: _____

Topic of Study: _____

Resources/References: _____
_____
_____
_____
_____

Pictures/Diagrams/Notes:

Key Thoughts/Learning:

_____
_____
_____
_____

Key Thoughts/Learning (cont.):

_____
_____
_____
_____
_____
_____
_____
_____
_____

On a scale of 1-10 (10 being the best), how well are you applying the topic of study already? _____

How can I apply these thoughts and concepts today and consistently in the future?

_____
_____
_____
_____

End-of-Day Evaluation:

Rate yourself on how much you improved? _____

Small step achieved today: _____

_____
_____
_____
_____

Did today matter? _____

I am grateful for _____

Page _____

Date/Time: _____

Location: _____

Topic of Study: _____

Resources/References: _____
_____
_____
_____
_____

Pictures/Diagrams/Notes:

Key Thoughts/Learning:

_____
_____
_____
_____

Key Thoughts/Learning (cont.):

_____

_____

_____

_____

_____

_____

_____

_____

_____

On a scale of 1-10 (10 being the best), how well are you applying the topic of study already? _____

How can I apply these thoughts and concepts today and consistently in the future?

_____

_____

_____

_____

End-of-Day Evaluation:

Rate yourself on how much you improved? _____

Small step achieved today: _____

_____

_____

_____

_____

Did today matter? _____

I am grateful for _____

Page _____

Date/Time: _____

Location: _____

Topic of Study: _____

Resources/References: _____

_____

_____

_____

_____

Pictures/Diagrams/Notes:

Key Thoughts/Learning:

_____

_____

_____

_____

Key Thoughts/Learning (cont.):

_____
_____
_____
_____
_____
_____
_____
_____
_____

On a scale of 1-10 (10 being the best), how well are you applying the topic of study already? _____

How can I apply these thoughts and concepts today and consistently in the future?

_____
_____
_____
_____

End-of-Day Evaluation:

Rate yourself on how much you improved? _____

Small step achieved today: _____
_____
_____
_____
_____

Did today matter? _____

I am grateful for _____

Page _____

Date/Time: _____

Location: _____

Topic of Study: _____

Resources/References: _____
_____
_____
_____
_____

Pictures/Diagrams/Notes:

Key Thoughts/Learning:

_____
_____
_____
_____

Key Thoughts/Learning (cont.):

_____
_____
_____
_____
_____
_____
_____
_____
_____

On a scale of 1-10 (10 being the best), how well are you applying the topic of study already? _____

How can I apply these thoughts and concepts today and consistently in the future?

_____
_____
_____
_____

End-of-Day Evaluation:

Rate yourself on how much you improved? _____

Small step achieved today: _____

_____
_____
_____
_____

Did today matter? _____

I am grateful for _____

Page _____

Date/Time: _____

Location: _____

Topic of Study: _____

Resources/References: _____

_____

_____

_____

_____

Pictures/Diagrams/Notes:

Key Thoughts/Learning:

_____

_____

_____

_____

Key Thoughts/Learning (cont.):

On a scale of 1-10 (10 being the best), how well are you applying the topic of study already? _____

How can I apply these thoughts and concepts today and consistently in the future?

End-of-Day Evaluation:

Rate yourself on how much you improved? _____

Small step achieved today: _____

Did today matter? _____

I am grateful for _____

Page _____

Date/Time: _____

Location: _____

Topic of Study: _____

Resources/References: _____
_____
_____
_____
_____

Pictures/Diagrams/Notes:

Key Thoughts/Learning:

_____
_____
_____
_____

Key Thoughts/Learning (cont.):

_____
_____
_____
_____
_____
_____
_____
_____
_____

On a scale of 1-10 (10 being the best), how well are you applying the topic of study already? _____

How can I apply these thoughts and concepts today and consistently in the future?

_____
_____
_____
_____

End-of-Day Evaluation:

Rate yourself on how much you improved? _____

Small step achieved today: _____

_____
_____
_____
_____

Did today matter? _____

I am grateful for _____

GIVE YOURSELF A GIFT...
THE GIFT OF GROWTH!

The Growth Mind
Academy

growthmindacademy.com

Page _____

Date/Time: _____

Location: _____

Topic of Study: _____

Resources/References: _____
_____
_____
_____
_____

Pictures/Diagrams/Notes:

Key Thoughts/Learning:

_____
_____
_____
_____

Key Thoughts/Learning (cont.):

_____
_____
_____
_____
_____
_____
_____
_____
_____

On a scale of 1-10 (10 being the best), how well are you applying the topic of study already? _____

How can I apply these thoughts and concepts today and consistently in the future?

_____
_____
_____
_____

End-of-Day Evaluation:

Rate yourself on how much you improved? _____

Small step achieved today: _____

_____
_____
_____
_____

Did today matter? _____

I am grateful for _____

Page _____

Date/Time: _____

Location: _____

Topic of Study: _____

Resources/References: _____
_____
_____
_____
_____

Pictures/Diagrams/Notes:

Key Thoughts/Learning:

_____
_____
_____
_____

Key Thoughts/Learning (cont.):

_____
_____
_____
_____
_____
_____
_____
_____
_____

On a scale of 1-10 (10 being the best), how well are you applying the topic of study already? _____

How can I apply these thoughts and concepts today and consistently in the future?

_____
_____
_____
_____

End-of-Day Evaluation:

Rate yourself on how much you improved? _____

Small step achieved today: _____

_____
_____
_____
_____

Did today matter? _____

I am grateful for _____

Page _____

Date/Time: _____

Location: _____

Topic of Study: _____

Resources/References: _____
_____
_____
_____
_____

Pictures/Diagrams/Notes:

Key Thoughts/Learning:

_____
_____
_____
_____

Key Thoughts/Learning (cont.):

_____
_____
_____
_____
_____
_____
_____
_____
_____

On a scale of 1-10 (10 being the best), how well are you applying the topic of study already? _____

How can I apply these thoughts and concepts today and consistently in the future?

_____
_____
_____
_____

End-of-Day Evaluation:

Rate yourself on how much you improved? _____

Small step achieved today: _____

_____
_____
_____
_____

Did today matter? _____

I am grateful for _____

Page _____

Date/Time: _____

Location: _____

Topic of Study: _____

Resources/References: _____

_____

_____

_____

_____

Pictures/Diagrams/Notes:

Key Thoughts/Learning:

_____

_____

_____

_____

Key Thoughts/Learning (cont.):

_____
_____
_____
_____
_____
_____
_____
_____
_____

On a scale of 1-10 (10 being the best), how well are you applying the topic of study already? _____

How can I apply these thoughts and concepts today and consistently in the future?

_____
_____
_____
_____

End-of-Day Evaluation:

Rate yourself on how much you improved? _____

Small step achieved today: _____
_____
_____
_____
_____

Did today matter? _____

I am grateful for _____

Page _____

Date/Time: _____

Location: _____

Topic of Study: _____

Resources/References: _____

_____

_____

_____

_____

Pictures/Diagrams/Notes:

Key Thoughts/Learning:

_____

_____

_____

_____

Key Thoughts/Learning (cont.):

_____
_____
_____
_____
_____
_____
_____
_____
_____

On a scale of 1-10 (10 being the best), how well are you applying the topic of study already? _____

How can I apply these thoughts and concepts today and consistently in the future?

_____
_____
_____
_____

End-of-Day Evaluation:

Rate yourself on how much you improved? _____

Small step achieved today: _____

_____
_____
_____
_____

Did today matter? _____

I am grateful for _____

Page _____

Date/Time: _____

Location: _____

Topic of Study: _____

Resources/References: _____
_____
_____
_____
_____

Pictures/Diagrams/Notes:

Key Thoughts/Learning:

_____
_____
_____
_____

Key Thoughts/Learning (cont.):

_____
_____
_____
_____
_____
_____
_____
_____
_____

On a scale of 1-10 (10 being the best), how well are you applying the topic of study already? _____

How can I apply these thoughts and concepts today and consistently in the future?

_____
_____
_____
_____

End-of-Day Evaluation:

Rate yourself on how much you improved? _____

Small step achieved today: _____

_____
_____
_____
_____

Did today matter? _____

I am grateful for _____

Page _____

Date/Time: _____

Location: _____

Topic of Study: _____

Resources/References: _____
_____
_____
_____
_____

Pictures/Diagrams/Notes:

Key Thoughts/Learning:

_____
_____
_____
_____

Key Thoughts/Learning (cont.):

_____
_____
_____
_____
_____
_____
_____
_____
_____

On a scale of 1-10 (10 being the best), how well are you applying the topic of study already? _____

How can I apply these thoughts and concepts today and consistently in the future?

_____
_____
_____
_____

End-of-Day Evaluation:

Rate yourself on how much you improved? _____

Small step achieved today: _____

_____
_____
_____
_____

Did today matter? _____

I am grateful for _____

Page _____

Date/Time: _____

Location: _____

Topic of Study: _____

Resources/References: _____
_____
_____
_____
_____

Pictures/Diagrams/Notes:

Key Thoughts/Learning:

_____
_____
_____
_____

Key Thoughts/Learning (cont.):

_____

_____

_____

_____

_____

_____

_____

_____

_____

On a scale of 1-10 (10 being the best), how well are you applying the topic of study already? _____

How can I apply these thoughts and concepts today and consistently in the future?

_____

_____

_____

_____

End-of-Day Evaluation:

Rate yourself on how much you improved? _____

Small step achieved today: _____

_____

_____

_____

_____

Did today matter? _____

I am grateful for _____

Page _____

Date/Time: _____

Location: _____

Topic of Study: _____

Resources/References: _____
_____
_____
_____
_____

Pictures/Diagrams/Notes:

Key Thoughts/Learning:

_____
_____
_____
_____

Key Thoughts/Learning (cont.):

_____
_____
_____
_____
_____
_____
_____
_____
_____

On a scale of 1-10 (10 being the best), how well are you applying the topic of study already? _____

How can I apply these thoughts and concepts today and consistently in the future?

_____
_____
_____
_____

End-of-Day Evaluation:

Rate yourself on how much you improved? _____

Small step achieved today: _____

_____
_____
_____
_____

Did today matter? _____

I am grateful for _____

Page _____

Date/Time: _____

Location: _____

Topic of Study: _____

Resources/References: _____

_____

_____

_____

_____

Pictures/Diagrams/Notes:

Key Thoughts/Learning:

_____

_____

_____

_____

Key Thoughts/Learning (cont.):

_____
_____
_____
_____
_____
_____
_____
_____
_____

On a scale of 1-10 (10 being the best), how well are you applying the topic of study already? _____

How can I apply these thoughts and concepts today and consistently in the future?

_____
_____
_____
_____

End-of-Day Evaluation:

Rate yourself on how much you improved? _____

Small step achieved today: _____

_____
_____
_____
_____

Did today matter? _____

I am grateful for _____

Page _____

Date/Time: _____

Location: _____

Topic of Study: _____

Resources/References: _____
_____
_____
_____
_____

Pictures/Diagrams/Notes:

Key Thoughts/Learning:

_____
_____
_____
_____

Key Thoughts/Learning (cont.):

_____
_____
_____
_____
_____
_____
_____
_____
_____

On a scale of 1-10 (10 being the best), how well are you applying the topic of study already? _____

How can I apply these thoughts and concepts today and consistently in the future?

_____
_____
_____
_____

End-of-Day Evaluation:

Rate yourself on how much you improved? _____

Small step achieved today: _____

_____
_____
_____
_____

Did today matter? _____

I am grateful for _____

Page _____

Date/Time: _____

Location: _____

Topic of Study: _____

Resources/References: _____
_____
_____
_____
_____

Pictures/Diagrams/Notes:

Key Thoughts/Learning:

_____
_____
_____
_____

Key Thoughts/Learning (cont.):

_____
_____
_____
_____
_____
_____
_____
_____
_____

On a scale of 1-10 (10 being the best), how well are you applying the topic of study already? _____

How can I apply these thoughts and concepts today and consistently in the future?

_____
_____
_____
_____

End-of-Day Evaluation:

Rate yourself on how much you improved? _____

Small step achieved today: _____
_____
_____
_____
_____

Did today matter? _____

I am grateful for _____

Page _____

Date/Time: _____

Location: _____

Topic of Study: _____

Resources/References: _____

_____

_____

_____

_____

Pictures/Diagrams/Notes:

Key Thoughts/Learning:

_____

_____

_____

_____

Key Thoughts/Learning (cont.):

_____
_____
_____
_____
_____
_____
_____
_____
_____

On a scale of 1-10 (10 being the best), how well are you applying the topic of study already? _____

How can I apply these thoughts and concepts today and consistently in the future?

_____
_____
_____
_____

End-of-Day Evaluation:

Rate yourself on how much you improved? _____

Small step achieved today: _____

_____
_____
_____
_____

Did today matter? _____

I am grateful for _____

Page _____

Date/Time: _____

Location: _____

Topic of Study: _____

Resources/References: _____
_____
_____
_____
_____

Pictures/Diagrams/Notes:

Key Thoughts/Learning:

_____
_____
_____
_____

Key Thoughts/Learning (cont.):

_____
_____
_____
_____
_____
_____
_____
_____
_____

On a scale of 1-10 (10 being the best), how well are you applying the topic of study already? _____

How can I apply these thoughts and concepts today and consistently in the future?

_____
_____
_____
_____

End-of-Day Evaluation:

Rate yourself on how much you improved? _____

Small step achieved today: _____

_____
_____
_____
_____

Did today matter? _____

I am grateful for _____

30-Day Check Point

On a scale of 1-10, how is your progress going? ____

Reflect on the last 30 days. What's working for you? What topics have you covered and grown in?

_____

_____

_____

_____

_____

_____

_____

_____

_____

_____

_____

_____

_____

_____

_____

_____

_____

_____

_____

_____

_____

_____

_____

_____

Page _____

Date/Time: _____

Location: _____

Topic of Study: _____

Resources/References: _____
_____
_____
_____
_____

Pictures/Diagrams/Notes:

Key Thoughts/Learning:

_____
_____
_____
_____

Key Thoughts/Learning (cont.):

_____
_____
_____
_____
_____
_____
_____
_____
_____

On a scale of 1-10 (10 being the best), how well are you applying the topic of study already? _____

How can I apply these thoughts and concepts today and consistently in the future?

_____
_____
_____
_____

End-of-Day Evaluation:

Rate yourself on how much you improved? _____

Small step achieved today: _____

_____
_____
_____
_____

Did today matter? _____

I am grateful for _____

Page _____

Date/Time: _____

Location: _____

Topic of Study: _____

Resources/References: _____
_____
_____
_____
_____

Pictures/Diagrams/Notes:

Key Thoughts/Learning:

_____
_____
_____
_____

Key Thoughts/Learning (cont.):

_____
_____
_____
_____
_____
_____
_____
_____
_____

On a scale of 1-10 (10 being the best), how well are you applying the topic of study already? _____

How can I apply these thoughts and concepts today and consistently in the future?

_____
_____
_____
_____

End-of-Day Evaluation:

Rate yourself on how much you improved? _____

Small step achieved today: _____

_____
_____
_____
_____

Did today matter? _____

I am grateful for _____

Page _____

Date/Time: _____

Location: _____

Topic of Study: _____

Resources/References: _____
_____
_____
_____
_____

Pictures/Diagrams/Notes:

Key Thoughts/Learning:

_____
_____
_____
_____

Key Thoughts/Learning (cont.):

_____
_____
_____
_____
_____
_____
_____
_____
_____

On a scale of 1-10 (10 being the best), how well are you applying the topic of study already? _____

How can I apply these thoughts and concepts today and consistently in the future?

_____
_____
_____
_____

End-of-Day Evaluation:

Rate yourself on how much you improved? _____

Small step achieved today: _____
_____
_____
_____
_____

Did today matter? _____

I am grateful for _____

Page _____

Date/Time: _____

Location: _____

Topic of Study: _____

Resources/References: _____
_____
_____
_____
_____

Pictures/Diagrams/Notes:

Key Thoughts/Learning:

_____
_____
_____
_____

Key Thoughts/Learning (cont.):

_____

_____

_____

_____

_____

_____

_____

_____

On a scale of 1-10 (10 being the best), how well are you applying the topic of study already? _____

How can I apply these thoughts and concepts today and consistently in the future?

_____

_____

_____

_____

End-of-Day Evaluation:

Rate yourself on how much you improved? _____

Small step achieved today: _____

_____

_____

_____

_____

Did today matter? _____

I am grateful for _____

Page _____

Date/Time: _____

Location: _____

Topic of Study: _____

Resources/References: _____
_____
_____
_____
_____

Pictures/Diagrams/Notes:

Key Thoughts/Learning:

_____
_____
_____
_____

Key Thoughts/Learning (cont.):

_____
_____
_____
_____
_____
_____
_____
_____
_____

On a scale of 1-10 (10 being the best), how well are you applying the topic of study already? _____

How can I apply these thoughts and concepts today and consistently in the future?

_____
_____
_____
_____

End-of-Day Evaluation:

Rate yourself on how much you improved? _____

Small step achieved today: _____
_____
_____
_____
_____

Did today matter? _____

I am grateful for _____

Page _____

Date/Time: _____

Location: _____

Topic of Study: _____

Resources/References: _____
_____
_____
_____
_____

Pictures/Diagrams/Notes:

Key Thoughts/Learning:

_____
_____
_____
_____

Key Thoughts/Learning (cont.):

_____
_____
_____
_____
_____
_____
_____
_____
_____

On a scale of 1-10 (10 being the best), how well are you applying the topic of study already? _____

How can I apply these thoughts and concepts today and consistently in the future?

_____
_____
_____
_____

End-of-Day Evaluation:

Rate yourself on how much you improved? _____

Small step achieved today: _____
_____
_____
_____
_____

Did today matter? _____

I am grateful for _____

Page _____

Date/Time: _____

Location: _____

Topic of Study: _____

Resources/References: _____
_____
_____
_____
_____

Pictures/Diagrams/Notes:

Key Thoughts/Learning:

_____
_____
_____
_____

Key Thoughts/Learning (cont.):

On a scale of 1-10 (10 being the best), how well are you applying the topic of study already? _____

How can I apply these thoughts and concepts today and consistently in the future?

End-of-Day Evaluation:

Rate yourself on how much you improved? _____

Small step achieved today: _____

Did today matter? _____

I am grateful for _____

Page _____

Date/Time: _____

Location: _____

Topic of Study: _____

Resources/References: _____

_____

_____

_____

_____

Pictures/Diagrams/Notes:

Key Thoughts/Learning:

_____

_____

_____

_____

Key Thoughts/Learning (cont.):

_____
_____
_____
_____
_____
_____
_____
_____
_____

On a scale of 1-10 (10 being the best), how well are you applying the topic of study already? _____

How can I apply these thoughts and concepts today and consistently in the future?

_____
_____
_____
_____

End-of-Day Evaluation:

Rate yourself on how much you improved? _____

Small step achieved today: _____

_____
_____
_____
_____

Did today matter? _____

I am grateful for _____

Page _____

Date/Time: _____

Location: _____

Topic of Study: _____

Resources/References: _____
_____
_____
_____
_____

Pictures/Diagrams/Notes:

Key Thoughts/Learning:

_____
_____
_____
_____

Key Thoughts/Learning (cont.):

_____
_____
_____
_____
_____
_____
_____
_____
_____

On a scale of 1-10 (10 being the best), how well are you applying the topic of study already? _____

How can I apply these thoughts and concepts today and consistently in the future?

_____
_____
_____
_____

End-of-Day Evaluation:

Rate yourself on how much you improved? _____

Small step achieved today: _____

_____
_____
_____
_____

Did today matter? _____

I am grateful for _____

Page _____

Date/Time: _____

Location: _____

Topic of Study: _____

Resources/References: _____

_____

_____

_____

_____

Pictures/Diagrams/Notes:

Key Thoughts/Learning:

_____

_____

_____

_____

Key Thoughts/Learning (cont.):

_____
_____
_____
_____
_____
_____
_____
_____
_____

On a scale of 1-10 (10 being the best), how well are you applying the topic of study already? _____

How can I apply these thoughts and concepts today and consistently in the future?

_____
_____
_____
_____

End-of-Day Evaluation:

Rate yourself on how much you improved? _____

Small step achieved today: _____

_____
_____
_____
_____

Did today matter? _____

I am grateful for _____

Page _____

Date/Time: _____

Location: _____

Topic of Study: _____

Resources/References: _____
_____
_____
_____
_____

Pictures/Diagrams/Notes:

Key Thoughts/Learning:

_____
_____
_____
_____

Key Thoughts/Learning (cont.):

_____
_____
_____
_____
_____
_____
_____
_____
_____

On a scale of 1-10 (10 being the best), how well are you applying the topic of study already? _____

How can I apply these thoughts and concepts today and consistently in the future?

_____
_____
_____
_____

End-of-Day Evaluation:

Rate yourself on how much you improved? _____

Small step achieved today: _____

_____
_____
_____
_____

Did today matter? _____

I am grateful for _____

Page _____

Date/Time: _____

Location: _____

Topic of Study: _____

Resources/References: _____
_____
_____
_____
_____

Pictures/Diagrams/Notes:

Key Thoughts/Learning:

_____
_____
_____
_____

Key Thoughts/Learning (cont.):

_____
_____
_____
_____
_____
_____
_____
_____
_____

On a scale of 1-10 (10 being the best), how well are you applying the
topic of study already? _____

How can I apply these thoughts and concepts today and consistently
in the future?

_____
_____
_____
_____

End-of-Day Evaluation:

Rate yourself on how much you improved? _____

Small step achieved today: _____

_____
_____
_____
_____

Did today matter? _____

I am grateful for _____

Page _____

Date/Time: _____

Location: _____

Topic of Study: _____

Resources/References: _____
_____
_____
_____
_____

Pictures/Diagrams/Notes:

Key Thoughts/Learning:

_____
_____
_____
_____

Key Thoughts/Learning (cont.):

_____
_____
_____
_____
_____
_____
_____
_____
_____

On a scale of 1-10 (10 being the best), how well are you applying the topic of study already? _____

How can I apply these thoughts and concepts today and consistently in the future?

_____
_____
_____
_____

End-of-Day Evaluation:

Rate yourself on how much you improved? _____

Small step achieved today: _____

_____
_____
_____
_____

Did today matter? _____

I am grateful for _____

Page _____

Date/Time: _____

Location: _____

Topic of Study: _____

Resources/References: _____
_____
_____
_____
_____

Pictures/Diagrams/Notes:

Key Thoughts/Learning:

_____
_____
_____
_____

Key Thoughts/Learning (cont.):

_____
_____
_____
_____
_____
_____
_____
_____
_____

On a scale of 1-10 (10 being the best), how well are you applying the topic of study already? _____

How can I apply these thoughts and concepts today and consistently in the future?

_____
_____
_____
_____

End-of-Day Evaluation:

Rate yourself on how much you improved? _____

Small step achieved today: _____

_____
_____
_____
_____

Did today matter? _____

I am grateful for _____

Page _____

Date/Time: _____

Location: _____

Topic of Study: _____

Resources/References: _____
_____
_____
_____
_____

Pictures/Diagrams/Notes:

Key Thoughts/Learning:

_____
_____
_____
_____

Key Thoughts/Learning (cont.):

On a scale of 1-10 (10 being the best), how well are you applying the topic of study already? _____

How can I apply these thoughts and concepts today and consistently in the future?

End-of-Day Evaluation:

Rate yourself on how much you improved? _____

Small step achieved today: _____

Did today matter? _____

I am grateful for _____

IT IS TIME TO

LIVE COMPLETE

and care for your whole self

-RICH IN WELLNESS STUDIO-
WWW.RIWSTUDIO.COM

Page _____

Date/Time: _____

Location: _____

Topic of Study: _____

Resources/References: _____

_____

_____

_____

_____

Pictures/Diagrams/Notes:

Key Thoughts/Learning:

_____

_____

_____

_____

Key Thoughts/Learning (cont.):

_____
_____
_____
_____
_____
_____
_____
_____
_____

On a scale of 1-10 (10 being the best), how well are you applying the topic of study already? _____

How can I apply these thoughts and concepts today and consistently in the future?

_____
_____
_____
_____

End-of-Day Evaluation:

Rate yourself on how much you improved? _____

Small step achieved today: _____

_____
_____
_____
_____

Did today matter? _____

I am grateful for _____

Page _____

Date/Time: _____

Location: _____

Topic of Study: _____

Resources/References: _____
_____
_____
_____
_____

Pictures/Diagrams/Notes:

Key Thoughts/Learning:

_____
_____
_____
_____

Key Thoughts/Learning (cont.):

_____
_____
_____
_____
_____
_____
_____
_____
_____

On a scale of 1-10 (10 being the best), how well are you applying the topic of study already? _____

How can I apply these thoughts and concepts today and consistently in the future?

_____
_____
_____
_____

End-of-Day Evaluation:

Rate yourself on how much you improved? _____

Small step achieved today: _____

_____
_____
_____
_____

Did today matter? _____

I am grateful for _____

Page _____

Date/Time: _____

Location: _____

Topic of Study: _____

Resources/References: _____

_____

_____

_____

_____

Pictures/Diagrams/Notes:

Key Thoughts/Learning:

_____

_____

_____

_____

Key Thoughts/Learning (cont.):

_____
_____
_____
_____
_____
_____
_____
_____
_____

On a scale of 1-10 (10 being the best), how well are you applying the topic of study already? _____

How can I apply these thoughts and concepts today and consistently in the future?

_____
_____
_____
_____

End-of-Day Evaluation:

Rate yourself on how much you improved? _____

Small step achieved today: _____
_____
_____
_____
_____

Did today matter? _____

I am grateful for _____

Page _____

Date/Time: _____

Location: _____

Topic of Study: _____

Resources/References: _____

_____

_____

_____

_____

Pictures/Diagrams/Notes:

Key Thoughts/Learning:

_____

_____

_____

_____

Key Thoughts/Learning (cont.):

_____
_____
_____
_____
_____
_____
_____
_____
_____

On a scale of 1-10 (10 being the best), how well are you applying the topic of study already? _____

How can I apply these thoughts and concepts today and consistently in the future?

_____
_____
_____
_____

End-of-Day Evaluation:

Rate yourself on how much you improved? _____

Small step achieved today: _____
_____
_____
_____
_____

Did today matter? _____

I am grateful for _____

Page _____

Date/Time: _____

Location: _____

Topic of Study: _____

Resources/References: _____
_____
_____
_____
_____

Pictures/Diagrams/Notes:

Key Thoughts/Learning:

_____
_____
_____
_____

Key Thoughts/Learning (cont.):

_____
_____
_____
_____
_____
_____
_____
_____
_____

On a scale of 1-10 (10 being the best), how well are you applying the topic of study already? _____

How can I apply these thoughts and concepts today and consistently in the future?

_____
_____
_____
_____

End-of-Day Evaluation:

Rate yourself on how much you improved? _____

Small step achieved today: _____

_____
_____
_____
_____

Did today matter? _____

I am grateful for _____

Page _____

Date/Time: _____

Location: _____

Topic of Study: _____

Resources/References: _____
_____
_____
_____
_____

Pictures/Diagrams/Notes:

Key Thoughts/Learning:

_____
_____
_____
_____

Key Thoughts/Learning (cont.):

_____
_____
_____
_____
_____
_____
_____
_____

On a scale of 1-10 (10 being the best), how well are you applying the topic of study already? _____

How can I apply these thoughts and concepts today and consistently in the future?

_____
_____
_____
_____

End-of-Day Evaluation:

Rate yourself on how much you improved? _____

Small step achieved today: _____

_____
_____
_____
_____

Did today matter? _____

I am grateful for _____

Page _____

Date/Time: _____

Location: _____

Topic of Study: _____

Resources/References: _____

_____

_____

_____

_____

Pictures/Diagrams/Notes:

Key Thoughts/Learning:

_____

_____

_____

_____

Key Thoughts/Learning (cont.):

_____
_____
_____
_____
_____
_____
_____
_____
_____

On a scale of 1-10 (10 being the best), how well are you applying the topic of study already? _____

How can I apply these thoughts and concepts today and consistently in the future?

_____
_____
_____
_____

End-of-Day Evaluation:

Rate yourself on how much you improved? _____

Small step achieved today: _____
_____
_____
_____
_____

Did today matter? _____

I am grateful for _____

Page _____

Date/Time: _____

Location: _____

Topic of Study: _____

Resources/References: _____
_____
_____
_____
_____

Pictures/Diagrams/Notes:

Key Thoughts/Learning:

_____
_____
_____
_____

Key Thoughts/Learning (cont.):

_____
_____
_____
_____
_____
_____
_____
_____
_____

On a scale of 1-10 (10 being the best), how well are you applying the topic of study already? _____

How can I apply these thoughts and concepts today and consistently in the future?

_____
_____
_____
_____

End-of-Day Evaluation:

Rate yourself on how much you improved? _____

Small step achieved today: _____

_____
_____
_____
_____

Did today matter? _____

I am grateful for _____

Page _____

Date/Time: _____

Location: _____

Topic of Study: _____

Resources/References: _____
_____
_____
_____
_____

Pictures/Diagrams/Notes:

Key Thoughts/Learning:

_____
_____
_____
_____

Key Thoughts/Learning (cont.):

_____
_____
_____
_____
_____
_____
_____
_____
_____

On a scale of 1-10 (10 being the best), how well are you applying the topic of study already? _____

How can I apply these thoughts and concepts today and consistently in the future?

_____
_____
_____
_____

End-of-Day Evaluation:

Rate yourself on how much you improved? _____

Small step achieved today: _____
_____
_____
_____
_____

Did today matter? _____

I am grateful for _____

Page _____

Date/Time: _____

Location: _____

Topic of Study: _____

Resources/References: _____
_____
_____
_____
_____

Pictures/Diagrams/Notes:

Key Thoughts/Learning:

_____
_____
_____
_____

Key Thoughts/Learning (cont.):

_____
_____
_____
_____
_____
_____
_____
_____
_____

On a scale of 1-10 (10 being the best), how well are you applying the topic of study already? _____

How can I apply these thoughts and concepts today and consistently in the future?

_____
_____
_____
_____

End-of-Day Evaluation:

Rate yourself on how much you improved? _____

Small step achieved today: _____

_____
_____
_____
_____

Did today matter? _____

I am grateful for _____

Page _____

Date/Time: _____

Location: _____

Topic of Study: _____

Resources/References: _____
_____
_____
_____
_____

Pictures/Diagrams/Notes:

Key Thoughts/Learning:

_____
_____
_____
_____

Key Thoughts/Learning (cont.):

_____
_____
_____
_____
_____
_____
_____
_____
_____

On a scale of 1-10 (10 being the best), how well are you applying the topic of study already? _____

How can I apply these thoughts and concepts today and consistently in the future?

_____
_____
_____
_____

End-of-Day Evaluation:

Rate yourself on how much you improved? _____

Small step achieved today: _____

_____
_____
_____
_____

Did today matter? _____

I am grateful for _____

Page _____

Date/Time: _____

Location: _____

Topic of Study: _____

Resources/References: _____
_____
_____
_____
_____

Pictures/Diagrams/Notes:

Key Thoughts/Learning:

_____
_____
_____
_____

Key Thoughts/Learning (cont.):

_____
_____
_____
_____
_____
_____
_____
_____
_____

On a scale of 1-10 (10 being the best), how well are you applying the topic of study already? _____

How can I apply these thoughts and concepts today and consistently in the future?

_____
_____
_____
_____

End-of-Day Evaluation:

Rate yourself on how much you improved? _____

Small step achieved today: _____

_____
_____
_____
_____

Did today matter? _____

I am grateful for _____

Page _____

Date/Time: _____

Location: _____

Topic of Study: _____

Resources/References: _____
_____
_____
_____
_____

Pictures/Diagrams/Notes:

Key Thoughts/Learning:

_____
_____
_____
_____

Key Thoughts/Learning (cont.):

_____
_____
_____
_____
_____
_____
_____
_____
_____

On a scale of 1-10 (10 being the best), how well are you applying the topic of study already? _____

How can I apply these thoughts and concepts today and consistently in the future?

_____
_____
_____
_____

End-of-Day Evaluation:

Rate yourself on how much you improved? _____

Small step achieved today: _____

_____
_____
_____
_____

Did today matter? _____

I am grateful for _____

Page _____

Date/Time: _____

Location: _____

Topic of Study: _____

Resources/References: _____
_____
_____
_____
_____

Pictures/Diagrams/Notes:

Key Thoughts/Learning:

_____
_____
_____
_____

Key Thoughts/Learning (cont.):

_____
_____
_____
_____
_____
_____
_____
_____
_____

On a scale of 1-10 (10 being the best), how well are you applying the topic of study already? _____

How can I apply these thoughts and concepts today and consistently in the future?

_____
_____
_____
_____

End-of-Day Evaluation:

Rate yourself on how much you improved? _____

Small step achieved today: _____

_____
_____
_____
_____

Did today matter? _____

I am grateful for _____

Page _____

Date/Time: _____

Location: _____

Topic of Study: _____

Resources/References: _____
_____
_____
_____
_____

Pictures/Diagrams/Notes:

Key Thoughts/Learning:

_____
_____
_____
_____

Key Thoughts/Learning (cont.):

_____
_____
_____
_____
_____
_____
_____
_____
_____

On a scale of 1-10 (10 being the best), how well are you applying the topic of study already? _____

How can I apply these thoughts and concepts today and consistently in the future?

_____
_____
_____
_____

End-of-Day Evaluation:

Rate yourself on how much you improved? _____

Small step achieved today: _____
_____
_____
_____
_____

Did today matter? _____

I am grateful for _____

30-Day Check Point

On a scale of 1-10, how is your progress going? ____

Reflect on the last 30 days. What's working for you? What topics have you covered and grown in? What changes in your life have you noticed from the last 60 days?

_____
_____
_____
_____
_____
_____
_____
_____
_____
_____
_____
_____
_____
_____
_____
_____
_____
_____
_____
_____
_____

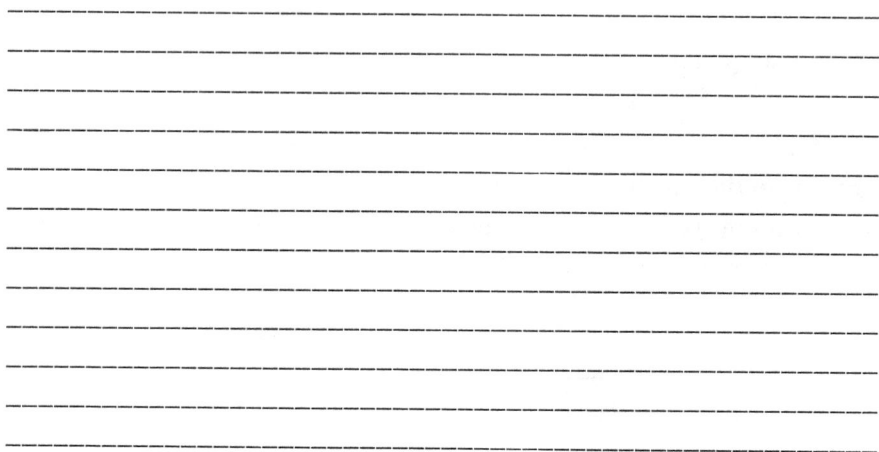

Page _____

Date/Time: _____

Location: _____

Topic of Study: _____

Resources/References: _____
_____
_____
_____
_____

Pictures/Diagrams/Notes:

Key Thoughts/Learning:

_____
_____
_____
_____

Key Thoughts/Learning (cont.):

_____
_____
_____
_____
_____
_____
_____
_____
_____

On a scale of 1-10 (10 being the best), how well are you applying the topic of study already? _____

How can I apply these thoughts and concepts today and consistently in the future?

_____
_____
_____
_____

End-of-Day Evaluation:

Rate yourself on how much you improved? _____

Small step achieved today: _____

_____
_____
_____
_____

Did today matter? _____

I am grateful for _____

Page _____

Date/Time: _____

Location: _____

Topic of Study: _____

Resources/References: _____
_____
_____
_____
_____

Pictures/Diagrams/Notes:

Key Thoughts/Learning:

_____
_____
_____
_____

Key Thoughts/Learning (cont.):

_____
_____
_____
_____
_____
_____
_____
_____
_____

On a scale of 1-10 (10 being the best), how well are you applying the topic of study already? _____

How can I apply these thoughts and concepts today and consistently in the future?

_____
_____
_____
_____

End-of-Day Evaluation:

Rate yourself on how much you improved? _____

Small step achieved today: _____
_____
_____
_____
_____

Did today matter? _____

I am grateful for _____

Page _____

Date/Time: _____

Location: _____

Topic of Study: _____

Resources/References: _____
_____
_____
_____
_____

Pictures/Diagrams/Notes:

Key Thoughts/Learning:

_____
_____
_____
_____

Key Thoughts/Learning (cont.):

_____
_____
_____
_____
_____
_____
_____
_____
_____

On a scale of 1-10 (10 being the best), how well are you applying the topic of study already? _____

How can I apply these thoughts and concepts today and consistently in the future?

_____
_____
_____
_____

End-of-Day Evaluation:

Rate yourself on how much you improved? _____

Small step achieved today: _____

_____
_____
_____
_____

Did today matter? _____

I am grateful for _____

Page _____

Date/Time: _____

Location: _____

Topic of Study: _____

Resources/References: _____
_____
_____
_____
_____

Pictures/Diagrams/Notes:

Key Thoughts/Learning:

_____
_____
_____
_____

Key Thoughts/Learning (cont.):

On a scale of 1-10 (10 being the best), how well are you applying the topic of study already? _____

How can I apply these thoughts and concepts today and consistently in the future?

End-of-Day Evaluation:

Rate yourself on how much you improved? _____

Small step achieved today: _____

Did today matter? _____

I am grateful for _____

Page _____

Date/Time: _____

Location: _____

Topic of Study: _____

Resources/References: _____
_____
_____
_____
_____

Pictures/Diagrams/Notes:

Key Thoughts/Learning:

_____
_____
_____
_____

Key Thoughts/Learning (cont.):

_____
_____
_____
_____
_____
_____
_____
_____
_____

On a scale of 1-10 (10 being the best), how well are you applying the topic of study already? _____

How can I apply these thoughts and concepts today and consistently in the future?

_____
_____
_____
_____

End-of-Day Evaluation:

Rate yourself on how much you improved? _____

Small step achieved today: _____

_____
_____
_____
_____

Did today matter? _____

I am grateful for _____

Page _____

Date/Time: _____

Location: _____

Topic of Study: _____

Resources/References: _____

_____

_____

_____

_____

Pictures/Diagrams/Notes:

Key Thoughts/Learning:

_____

_____

_____

_____

Key Thoughts/Learning (cont.):

_____
_____
_____
_____
_____
_____
_____
_____
_____

On a scale of 1-10 (10 being the best), how well are you applying the topic of study already? _____

How can I apply these thoughts and concepts today and consistently in the future?

_____
_____
_____
_____

End-of-Day Evaluation:

Rate yourself on how much you improved? _____

Small step achieved today: _____

_____
_____
_____
_____

Did today matter? _____

I am grateful for _____

Page _____

Date/Time: _____

Location: _____

Topic of Study: _____

Resources/References: _____
_____
_____
_____
_____

Pictures/Diagrams/Notes:

Key Thoughts/Learning:

_____
_____
_____
_____

Key Thoughts/Learning (cont.):

_____
_____
_____
_____
_____
_____
_____
_____
_____

On a scale of 1-10 (10 being the best), how well are you applying the topic of study already? _____

How can I apply these thoughts and concepts today and consistently in the future?

_____
_____
_____
_____

End-of-Day Evaluation:

Rate yourself on how much you improved? _____

Small step achieved today: _____

_____
_____
_____
_____

Did today matter? _____

I am grateful for _____

Page _____

Date/Time: _____

Location: _____

Topic of Study: _____

Resources/References: _____
_____
_____
_____
_____

Pictures/Diagrams/Notes:

Key Thoughts/Learning:

_____
_____
_____
_____

Key Thoughts/Learning (cont.):

_____
_____
_____
_____
_____
_____
_____
_____
_____

On a scale of 1-10 (10 being the best), how well are you applying the topic of study already? _____

How can I apply these thoughts and concepts today and consistently in the future?

_____
_____
_____
_____

End-of-Day Evaluation:

Rate yourself on how much you improved? _____

Small step achieved today: _____

_____
_____
_____
_____

Did today matter? _____

I am grateful for _____

Page _____

Date/Time: _____

Location: _____

Topic of Study: _____

Resources/References: _____
_____
_____
_____
_____

Pictures/Diagrams/Notes:

Key Thoughts/Learning:
_____
_____
_____
_____

Key Thoughts/Learning (cont.):

_____
_____
_____
_____
_____
_____
_____
_____
_____

On a scale of 1-10 (10 being the best), how well are you applying the topic of study already? _____

How can I apply these thoughts and concepts today and consistently in the future?

_____
_____
_____
_____

End-of-Day Evaluation:

Rate yourself on how much you improved? _____

Small step achieved today: _____

_____
_____
_____
_____

Did today matter? _____

I am grateful for _____

Page _____

Date/Time: _____

Location: _____

Topic of Study: _____

Resources/References: _____
_____
_____
_____
_____

Pictures/Diagrams/Notes:

Key Thoughts/Learning:

_____
_____
_____
_____

Key Thoughts/Learning (cont.):

_____
_____
_____
_____
_____
_____
_____
_____
_____

On a scale of 1-10 (10 being the best), how well are you applying the topic of study already? _____

How can I apply these thoughts and concepts today and consistently in the future?

_____
_____
_____
_____

End-of-Day Evaluation:

Rate yourself on how much you improved? _____

Small step achieved today: _____

_____
_____
_____
_____

Did today matter? _____

I am grateful for _____

Page _____

Date/Time: _____

Location: _____

Topic of Study: _____

Resources/References: _____

_____

_____

_____

_____

Pictures/Diagrams/Notes:

Key Thoughts/Learning:

_____

_____

_____

_____

Key Thoughts/Learning (cont.):

On a scale of 1-10 (10 being the best), how well are you applying the topic of study already? _____

How can I apply these thoughts and concepts today and consistently in the future?

End-of-Day Evaluation:

Rate yourself on how much you improved? _____

Small step achieved today: _____

Did today matter? _____

I am grateful for _____

Page _____

Date/Time: _____

Location: _____

Topic of Study: _____

Resources/References: _____

_____

_____

_____

_____

Pictures/Diagrams/Notes:

Key Thoughts/Learning:

_____

_____

_____

_____

Key Thoughts/Learning (cont.):

_____
_____
_____
_____
_____
_____
_____
_____
_____

On a scale of 1-10 (10 being the best), how well are you applying the topic of study already? _____

How can I apply these thoughts and concepts today and consistently in the future?

_____
_____
_____
_____

End-of-Day Evaluation:

Rate yourself on how much you improved? _____

Small step achieved today: _____

_____
_____
_____
_____

Did today matter? _____

I am grateful for _____

Page _____

Date/Time: _____

Location: _____

Topic of Study: _____

Resources/References: _____

_____
_____
_____
_____

Pictures/Diagrams/Notes:

Key Thoughts/Learning:

_____
_____
_____
_____

Key Thoughts/Learning (cont.):

_____
_____
_____
_____
_____
_____
_____
_____
_____

On a scale of 1-10 (10 being the best), how well are you applying the topic of study already? _____

How can I apply these thoughts and concepts today and consistently in the future?

_____
_____
_____
_____

End-of-Day Evaluation:

Rate yourself on how much you improved? _____

Small step achieved today: _____

_____
_____
_____
_____

Did today matter? _____

I am grateful for _____

Page _____

Date/Time: _____

Location: _____

Topic of Study: _____

Resources/References: _____

_____

_____

_____

_____

Pictures/Diagrams/Notes:

Key Thoughts/Learning:

_____

_____

_____

_____

Key Thoughts/Learning (cont.):

On a scale of 1-10 (10 being the best), how well are you applying the topic of study already? _____

How can I apply these thoughts and concepts today and consistently in the future?

End-of-Day Evaluation:

Rate yourself on how much you improved? _____

Small step achieved today: _____

Did today matter? _____

I am grateful for _____

Page _____

Date/Time: _____

Location: _____

Topic of Study: _____

Resources/References: _____

_____

_____

_____

_____

Pictures/Diagrams/Notes:

Key Thoughts/Learning:

_____

_____

_____

_____

Key Thoughts/Learning (cont.):

_____
_____
_____
_____
_____
_____
_____
_____
_____

On a scale of 1-10 (10 being the best), how well are you applying the topic of study already? _____

How can I apply these thoughts and concepts today and consistently in the future?

_____
_____
_____
_____

End-of-Day Evaluation:

Rate yourself on how much you improved? _____

Small step achieved today: _____

_____
_____
_____
_____

Did today matter? _____

I am grateful for _____

CONSIDER THE
VALUE OF YOU

—

LET YOUR LIGHT
SHINE

—

WWW.RIWSTUDIO.COM

Page _____

Date/Time: _____

Location: _____

Topic of Study: _____

Resources/References: _____
_____
_____
_____
_____

Pictures/Diagrams/Notes:

Key Thoughts/Learning:

_____
_____
_____
_____

Key Thoughts/Learning (cont.):

_____

_____

_____

_____

_____

_____

_____

_____

_____

On a scale of 1-10 (10 being the best), how well are you applying the topic of study already? _____

How can I apply these thoughts and concepts today and consistently in the future?

_____

_____

_____

_____

End-of-Day Evaluation:

Rate yourself on how much you improved? _____

Small step achieved today: _____

_____

_____

_____

_____

Did today matter? _____

I am grateful for _____

Page _____

Date/Time: _____

Location: _____

Topic of Study: _____

Resources/References: _____
_____
_____
_____
_____

Pictures/Diagrams/Notes:

Key Thoughts/Learning:

_____
_____
_____
_____

Key Thoughts/Learning (cont.):

_____
_____
_____
_____
_____
_____
_____
_____
_____

On a scale of 1-10 (10 being the best), how well are you applying the topic of study already? _____

How can I apply these thoughts and concepts today and consistently in the future?

_____
_____
_____
_____

End-of-Day Evaluation:

Rate yourself on how much you improved? _____

Small step achieved today: _____

_____
_____
_____
_____

Did today matter? _____

I am grateful for _____

Page _____

Date/Time: _____

Location: _____

Topic of Study: _____

Resources/References: _____

_____

_____

_____

_____

Pictures/Diagrams/Notes:

Key Thoughts/Learning:

_____

_____

_____

_____

Key Thoughts/Learning (cont.):

_____
_____
_____
_____
_____
_____
_____
_____
_____

On a scale of 1-10 (10 being the best), how well are you applying the topic of study already? _____

How can I apply these thoughts and concepts today and consistently in the future?

_____
_____
_____
_____

End-of-Day Evaluation:

Rate yourself on how much you improved? _____

Small step achieved today: _____

_____
_____
_____
_____

Did today matter? _____

I am grateful for _____

Page _____

Date/Time: _____

Location: _____

Topic of Study: _____

Resources/References: _____
_____
_____
_____
_____

Pictures/Diagrams/Notes:

Key Thoughts/Learning:

_____
_____
_____
_____

Key Thoughts/Learning (cont.):

_____
_____
_____
_____
_____
_____
_____
_____
_____

On a scale of 1-10 (10 being the best), how well are you applying the topic of study already? _____

How can I apply these thoughts and concepts today and consistently in the future?

_____
_____
_____
_____

End-of-Day Evaluation:

Rate yourself on how much you improved? _____

Small step achieved today: _____
_____
_____
_____
_____

Did today matter? _____

I am grateful for _____

Page _____

Date/Time: _____

Location: _____

Topic of Study: _____

Resources/References: _____
_____
_____
_____
_____

Pictures/Diagrams/Notes:

Key Thoughts/Learning:

_____
_____
_____
_____

Key Thoughts/Learning (cont.):

_____
_____
_____
_____
_____
_____
_____
_____
_____

On a scale of 1-10 (10 being the best), how well are you applying the topic of study already? _____

How can I apply these thoughts and concepts today and consistently in the future?

_____
_____
_____
_____

End-of-Day Evaluation:

Rate yourself on how much you improved? _____

Small step achieved today: _____

_____
_____
_____
_____

Did today matter? _____

I am grateful for _____

Page _____

Date/Time: _____

Location: _____

Topic of Study: _____

Resources/References: _____
_____
_____
_____
_____

Pictures/Diagrams/Notes:

Key Thoughts/Learning:

_____
_____
_____
_____

Key Thoughts/Learning (cont.):

_____
_____
_____
_____
_____
_____
_____
_____
_____

On a scale of 1-10 (10 being the best), how well are you applying the topic of study already? _____

How can I apply these thoughts and concepts today and consistently in the future?

_____
_____
_____
_____

End-of-Day Evaluation:

Rate yourself on how much you improved? _____

Small step achieved today: _____

_____
_____
_____
_____

Did today matter? _____

I am grateful for _____

Page _____

Date/Time: _____

Location: _____

Topic of Study: _____

Resources/References: _____

_____
_____
_____
_____

Pictures/Diagrams/Notes:

Key Thoughts/Learning:

_____
_____
_____
_____

Key Thoughts/Learning (cont.):

_____
_____
_____
_____
_____
_____
_____
_____
_____

On a scale of 1-10 (10 being the best), how well are you applying the topic of study already? _____

How can I apply these thoughts and concepts today and consistently in the future?

_____
_____
_____
_____

End-of-Day Evaluation:

Rate yourself on how much you improved? _____

Small step achieved today: _____
_____
_____
_____
_____

Did today matter? _____

I am grateful for _____

Page _____

Date/Time: _____

Location: _____

Topic of Study: _____

Resources/References: _____
_____
_____
_____
_____

Pictures/Diagrams/Notes:

Key Thoughts/Learning:

_____
_____
_____
_____

Key Thoughts/Learning (cont.):

_____
_____
_____
_____
_____
_____
_____
_____
_____

On a scale of 1-10 (10 being the best), how well are you applying the topic of study already? _____

How can I apply these thoughts and concepts today and consistently in the future?

_____
_____
_____
_____

End-of-Day Evaluation:

Rate yourself on how much you improved? _____

Small step achieved today: _____
_____
_____
_____
_____

Did today matter? _____

I am grateful for _____

Page _____

Date/Time: _____

Location: _____

Topic of Study: _____

Resources/References: _____
_____
_____
_____
_____

Pictures/Diagrams/Notes:

Key Thoughts/Learning:

_____
_____
_____
_____

Key Thoughts/Learning (cont.):

_____
_____
_____
_____
_____
_____
_____
_____
_____

On a scale of 1-10 (10 being the best), how well are you applying the topic of study already? _____

How can I apply these thoughts and concepts today and consistently in the future?

_____
_____
_____
_____

End-of-Day Evaluation:

Rate yourself on how much you improved? _____

Small step achieved today: _____

_____
_____
_____
_____

Did today matter? _____

I am grateful for _____

Page _____

Date/Time: _____

Location: _____

Topic of Study: _____

Resources/References: _____
_____
_____
_____
_____

Pictures/Diagrams/Notes:

Key Thoughts/Learning:

_____
_____
_____
_____

Key Thoughts/Learning (cont.):

_____
_____
_____
_____
_____
_____
_____
_____
_____

On a scale of 1-10 (10 being the best), how well are you applying the topic of study already? _____

How can I apply these thoughts and concepts today and consistently in the future?

_____
_____
_____
_____

End-of-Day Evaluation:

Rate yourself on how much you improved? _____

Small step achieved today: _____

_____
_____
_____
_____

Did today matter? _____

I am grateful for _____

Page _____

Date/Time: _____

Location: _____

Topic of Study: _____

Resources/References: _____

_____

_____

_____

_____

Pictures/Diagrams/Notes:

Key Thoughts/Learning:

_____

_____

_____

_____

Key Thoughts/Learning (cont.):

_____
_____
_____
_____
_____
_____
_____
_____
_____

On a scale of 1-10 (10 being the best), how well are you applying the topic of study already? _____

How can I apply these thoughts and concepts today and consistently in the future?

_____
_____
_____
_____

End-of-Day Evaluation:

Rate yourself on how much you improved? _____

Small step achieved today: _____

_____
_____
_____
_____

Did today matter? _____

I am grateful for _____

Page _____

Date/Time: _____

Location: _____

Topic of Study: _____

Resources/References: _____
_____
_____
_____
_____

Pictures/Diagrams/Notes:

Key Thoughts/Learning:

_____
_____
_____
_____

Key Thoughts/Learning (cont.):

_____
_____
_____
_____
_____
_____
_____
_____
_____

On a scale of 1-10 (10 being the best), how well are you applying the topic of study already? _____

How can I apply these thoughts and concepts today and consistently in the future?

_____
_____
_____
_____

End-of-Day Evaluation:

Rate yourself on how much you improved? _____

Small step achieved today: _____

_____
_____
_____
_____

Did today matter? _____

I am grateful for _____

Page _____

Date/Time: _____

Location: _____

Topic of Study: _____

Resources/References: _____

_____

_____

_____

_____

Pictures/Diagrams/Notes:

Key Thoughts/Learning:

_____

_____

_____

_____

Key Thoughts/Learning (cont.):

_____
_____
_____
_____
_____
_____
_____
_____
_____

On a scale of 1-10 (10 being the best), how well are you applying the topic of study already? _____

How can I apply these thoughts and concepts today and consistently in the future?

_____
_____
_____
_____

End-of-Day Evaluation:

Rate yourself on how much you improved? _____

Small step achieved today: _____

_____
_____
_____
_____

Did today matter? _____

I am grateful for _____

Page _____

Date/Time: _____

Location: _____

Topic of Study: _____

Resources/References: _____
_____
_____
_____
_____

Pictures/Diagrams/Notes:

Key Thoughts/Learning:

_____
_____
_____
_____

Key Thoughts/Learning (cont.):

_____
_____
_____
_____
_____
_____
_____
_____
_____

On a scale of 1-10 (10 being the best), how well are you applying the topic of study already? _____

How can I apply these thoughts and concepts today and consistently in the future?

_____
_____
_____
_____

End-of-Day Evaluation:

Rate yourself on how much you improved? _____

Small step achieved today: _____

_____
_____
_____
_____

Did today matter? _____

I am grateful for _____

Page _____

Date/Time: _____

Location: _____

Topic of Study: _____

Resources/References: _____
_____
_____
_____
_____

Pictures/Diagrams/Notes:

Key Thoughts/Learning:

_____
_____
_____
_____

Key Thoughts/Learning (cont.):

_____
_____
_____
_____
_____
_____
_____
_____
_____

On a scale of 1-10 (10 being the best), how well are you applying the topic of study already? _____

How can I apply these thoughts and concepts today and consistently in the future?

_____
_____
_____
_____

End-of-Day Evaluation:

Rate yourself on how much you improved? _____

Small step achieved today: _____

_____
_____
_____
_____

Did today matter? _____

I am grateful for _____

30-Day Check Point

On a scale of 1-10, how is your progress going? ____

Reflect on the last 30 days. What topics have you covered and
grown in? What have you implemented from the last 60 days that
worked in the last 30 days? What changes have you seen in your life
as a result of your last 30 day growth?

_____
_____
_____
_____
_____
_____
_____
_____
_____
_____
_____
_____
_____
_____
_____
_____
_____
_____
_____
_____
_____

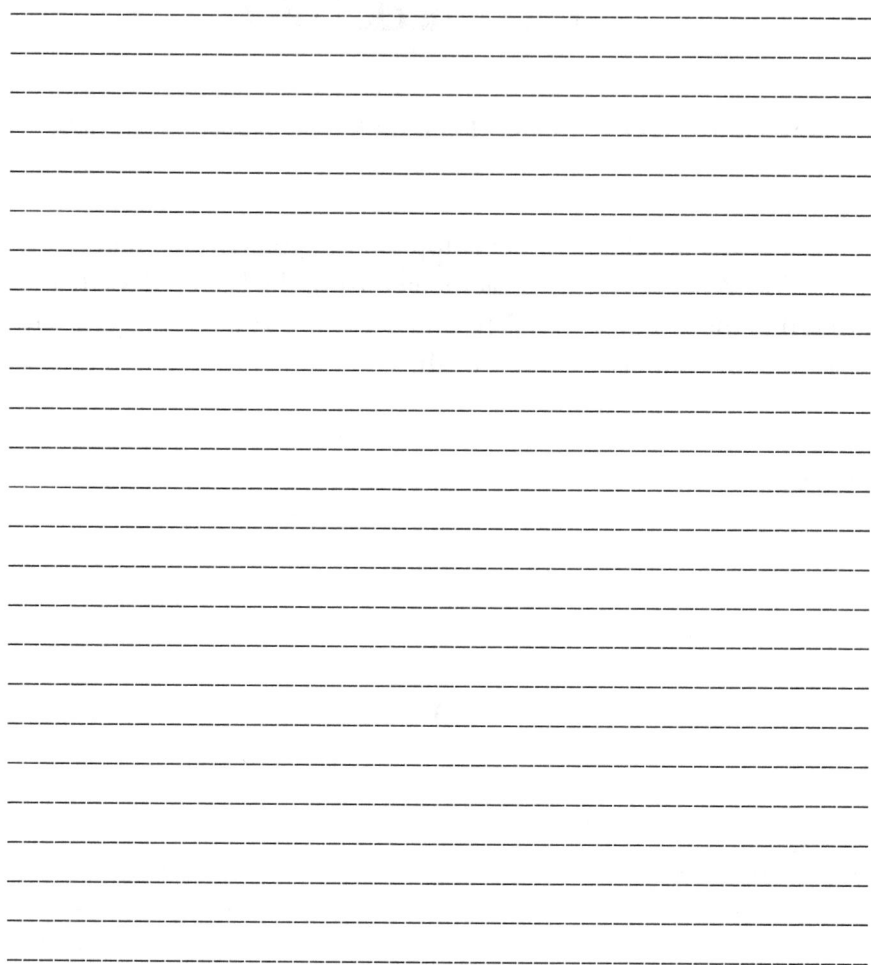

YOU DID IT!

YOU COMPLETED 90 DAYS OF PERSONAL GROWTH DEVELOPMENT!

As the final touches, go back through your journal and stop at any page that catches your attention. Reflect and draw/write about your journey on the following pages. Reflect on the changes you noticed about your life. Consider what you will do for your next 90 days! Celebrate your successful growth no matter where you are.

"Love the YOU that is still developing. We are not perfect and never will be. So just love you-the person that is taking the journey of life and growing."

-S. Kanani Haiola

ISBN 978-0-9965390-4-3

www.ingramcontent.com/pod-product-compliance
Lightning Source LLC
Chambersburg PA
CBHW070839100426
42813CB00003B/678